PIANO TIME PIECES
Book 2

28 companion pieces to Piano Time 2

new edition

Pauline Hall

MUSIC DEPARTMENT

OXFORD
UNIVERSITY PRESS

OXFORD
UNIVERSITY PRESS

Great Clarendon Street, Oxford OX2 6DP, England
198 Madison Avenue, New York, NY10016, USA

Oxford is a registered trade mark of Oxford University Press
in the UK and in certain other countries

© Oxford University Press 1989, 2004

The moral rights of the author have been asserted

Database right Oxford University Press (maker)

First published 1989
New edition 2004

ISBN 978-0-19-372787-8

Music and text origination by
Barnes Music Engraving Ltd., East Sussex
Printed in Great Britain on acid-free paper by
Halstan Ltd., Amersham, Bucks., England.

Copyright acknowledgements

Gypsy tango (p. 16) by Gerald Martin © copyright control.

You can't keep a horse in a lighthouse (p. 27): words and music by Billy Clarges,
Jack Hill, and Emile Littler. © 1937 B. Feldman & Co. Ltd, London WC2H 0QY.
Reproduced by permisson of IMP Ltd, 161 Hammersmith Road, London, W6
8BS. All rights reserved.

Contents

Minuet

Alexander Reinagle
(1756–1809)

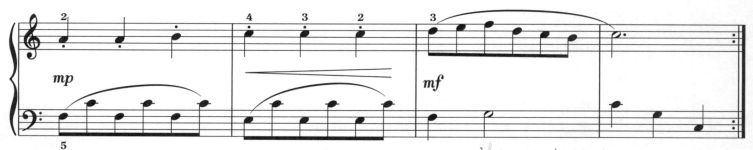

4

Breakfast time

Alan Bullard

Waltzing Matilda

Australian song
arr. Pauline Hall

Cheerfully

6

Tarantella

A Tarantella is a fast, whirling dance from Sicily. Dancing it was supposed to cure the bite of a tarantula spider.

Pauline Hall

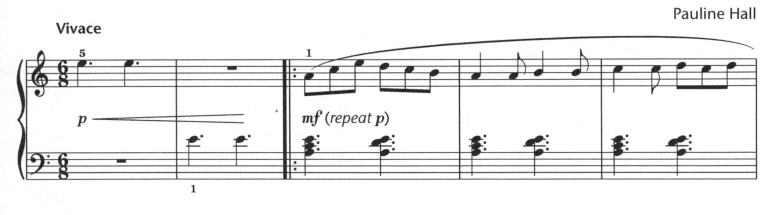

The little hedgehog

Notice that your left hand plays in the treble clef. You only need to use fingers 1, 3, and 5 in both hands. When thumbs play, they are always on next-door notes. Listen for the prickles–on the first quaver of every bar–ouch!

There are only three chords in this piece:

Left hand:  **Right hand:**

Dmitri Kabalevsky
(1904–87)

Russian carol

This carol should sound very bright and crisp.

arr. Pauline Hall

Moderato

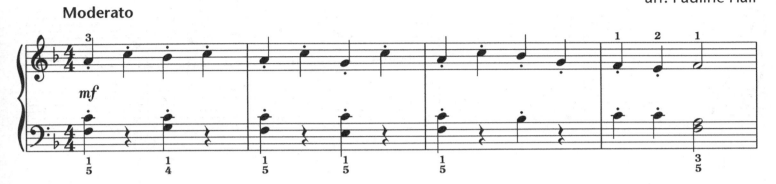

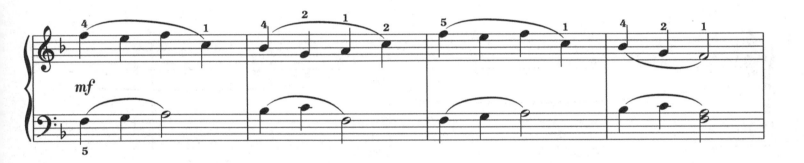

My bonnie lies over the ocean

Scottish traditional
arr. Pauline Hall

With a slow lilt

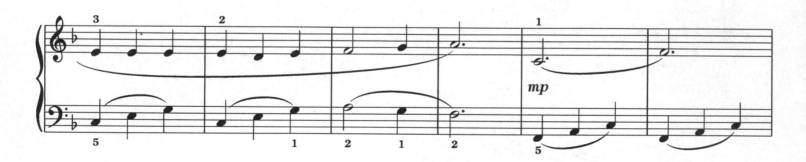

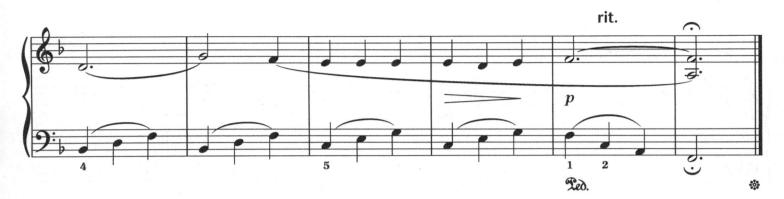

The wise elephant

David Blackwell

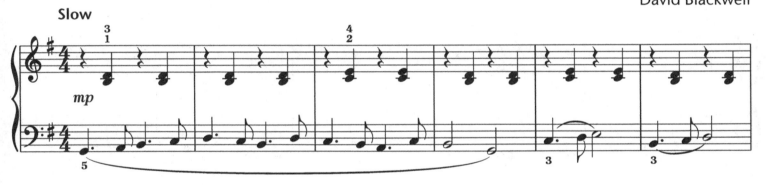

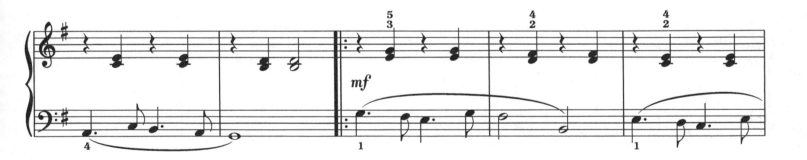

Feeling fine

Alan Bullard

Relaxed but rhythmic

Allegretto grazioso

Cornelius Gurlitt
(1820–1901)

Gavotte

James Hook
(1746–1827)

Allegretto

14

Auld lang syne

Scottish traditional

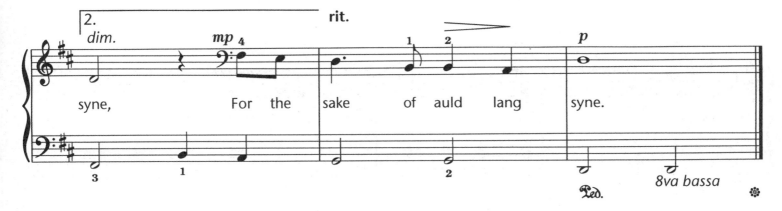

Gypsy tango

Gerald Martin

Moderately, with marked rhythm

Rattlesnake rag

Steadily

Pauline Hall

Climbing high

Alan Bullard

I hear a guitar

Hansi Alt

Five little frogs

L. B. Scott and Lucille Wood

Cheerfully

Five lit - tle spe-ckled frogs sat on a spe-ckled log, catch-ing some

most de - li - cious bugs, yum, yum! One jumped in - to the pool,

where it was nice and cool, and there were four green spe-ckled frogs, glub, glub!

21

Quadrille

Alexander Reinagle
(1756–1809)

Gigue

Olive J. Wood

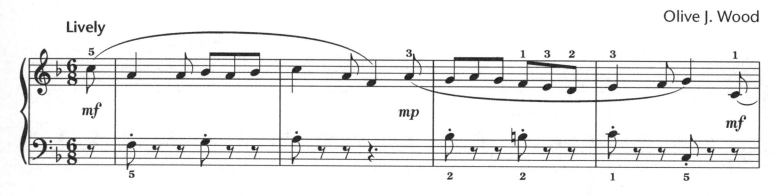

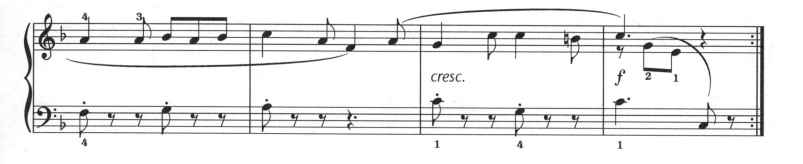

23

Russian winter

The sustaining pedal will help create the right atmosphere for this piece. Try pedalling once per bar.

David Blackwell

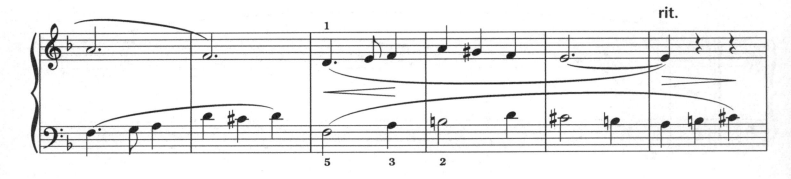

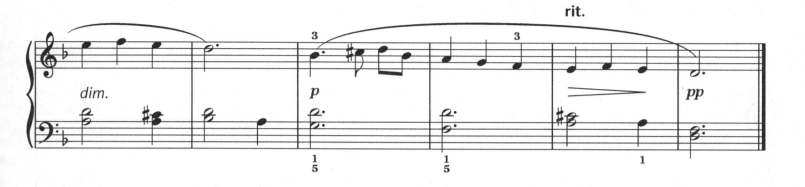

Swing low, sweet chariot

Spiritual
arr. Pauline Hall

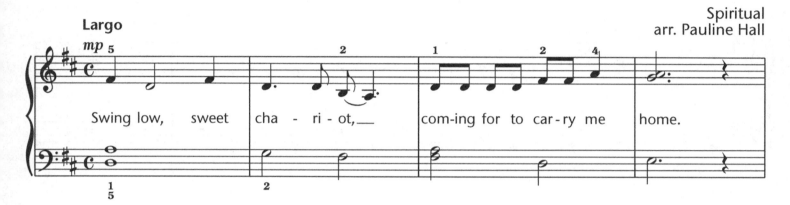

Swing low, sweet cha - ri - ot, __ com-ing for to car-ry me home.

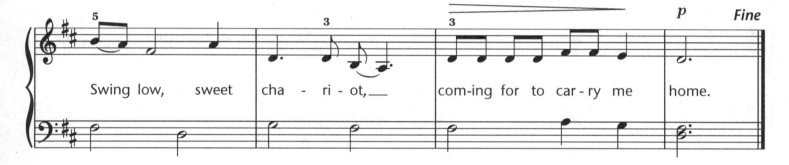

Swing low, sweet cha - ri - ot, __ com-ing for to car-ry me home.

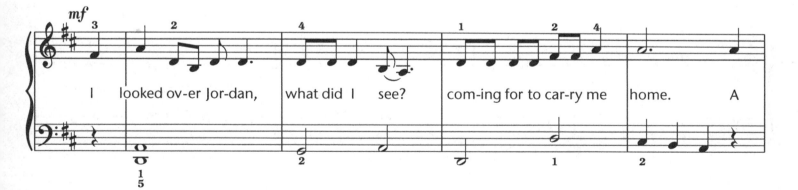

I looked ov-er Jor-dan, what did I see? com-ing for to car-ry me home. A

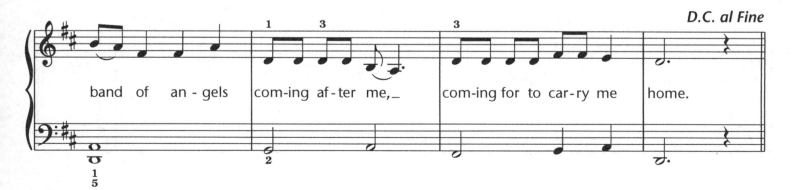

band of an - gels com-ing af-ter me, __ com-ing for to car-ry me home.

Grandmother's footsteps

Paul Drayton

On tiptoe

You can't keep a horse in a lighthouse

Clarges/Hill/Little
arr. Pauline Hall

The princess and the spinning-wheel

As the princess sits spinning, she dreams about dancing a waltz at a grand ball. Make your playing tell the story.

Pauline Hall

Holiday mood

David Blackwell

Try playing the right hand part an octave higher on the repeat.

Alabama bound

American railroad ballad
arr. Pauline Hall

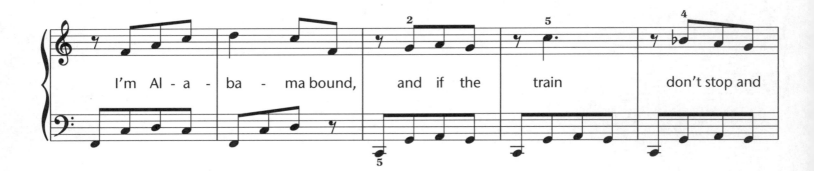

Valse triste

In waltz time

Robert Washburn

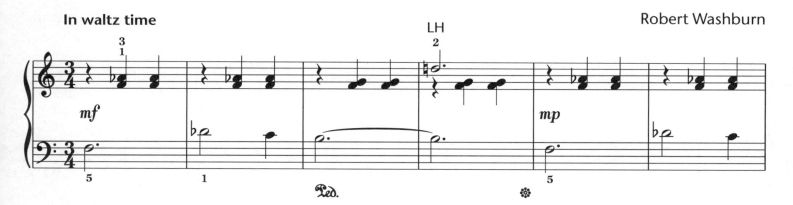

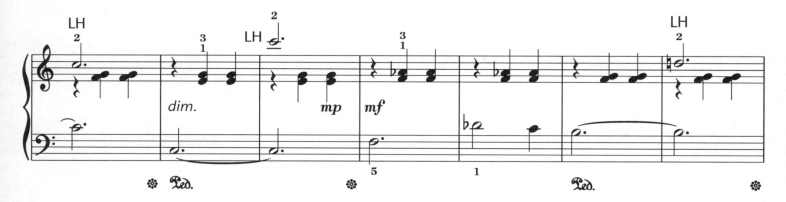

Rollercoaster ride

David Blackwell